# Clem
## and
# Nellie

An Unlikely Birds Tale

D. L. Burke

ISBN 979-8-88943-313-2 (paperback)
ISBN 979-8-89345-722-3 (hardcover)
ISBN 979-8-88943-314-9 (digital)

Copyright © 2024 by D. L. Burke

All rights reserved. No part of this publication may be reproduced, distributed, or transmitted in any form or by any means, including photocopying, recording, or other electronic or mechanical methods without the prior written permission of the publisher. For permission requests, solicit the publisher via the address below.

Christian Faith Publishing
832 Park Avenue
Meadville, PA 16335
www.christianfaithpublishing.com

Printed in the United States of America

In loving memory of my aunt Bonnie for nurturing my love of books and reading with countless trips to bookstores and libraries for as long as I can remember; for igniting my love of ducks that summer when I was six by letting me play with her rescued ducklings and then later letting me help release them at the park (to this day, the smell of duck ponds reminds me of that wonderful experience!); and for always praying for, encouraging, and loving me during the rough years.

She was my aunt, mom, mentor, and friend all rolled into one. I'm so grateful to have had her as my aunt, and I will miss her forever.

She always wanted to write a book but never got around to it, so this one's for her.


Thank you to God and to Grizzly the dog. This book would have never been written without the two of you.

One hot midsummer day, a kind-hearted man found a tiny duckling all alone in a bed of ivy.

He was covered with cobwebs and was really quite a mess!

The duckling seemed happy to be found and sat on the man's shoulder the rest of the day while he worked.

The kind-hearted man sent his wife a selfie of the two of them together and told her he was bringing the tiny duckling home.

The wife of the kind-hearted man (who, truth be told, was even kinder) was excited to hear the news, for she had always secretly wished for a duck of her very own!

She was so excited, she couldn't wait to tell her daughter (who was extra special and was the kindest of them all).

So together, the two of them set off to buy all the things a duckling would need.

The young man at the feed store told them the duckling would need a friend so it wouldn't be lonely.

The store was fresh out of baby ducks, so together, the lady and the girl who was extra special picked out a petite yellow chick to be the duckling's friend.

The chick was named Nellie (because she was very nervous), and the duckling they named Clementine (they call him Clem for short and to this day still aren't sure why they named him that!).

The extra special girl and the family dog loved to sit and watch the two birds chase each other around and play. They were so cute and funny!

The whole family (including the dog) was amazed by how fast the young birds grew! Before they knew it, their feathers had all changed, and they needed a bigger pen!

So on another hot day, the kind-hearted man and the lady built a super deluxe enclosure for the two birds. The man liked to call it their penthouse because it was so fancy!

It had plenty of room for them to run and play. There was a cozy house with two nests for egg-laying or sleeping, and it even had a pond for Clementine to swim in (as ducks very much like to swim!).

The birds were like brother and sister. One minute they would be fighting over a scrap of tomato or a worm, and the next, Nellie would sit in the mud next to Clem's pond so she could be near him (and everybody knows hens don't like to be wet). It was easy to see they were very fond of one another!

Taking care of the birds was a lot of work for the lady and the special girl. They had to clean the pen and then feed and water them at least twice a day (usually three times as the birds were quite spoiled!).

The lady would hold Clem on her lap many evenings, and the girl would giggle as he nibbled on her fingers. Sometimes he even went to sleep on the lady's chest. He very clearly loved his family! And they most definitely loved him!

Nellie began to lay eggs. This was very exciting for the extra special girl! Every day she would ask, "Did Nellie lay her egg today?" It never failed to make her smile when the lady would say yes and then show it to her.

The girl would always yell out, "Thank you, Nellie!"

The two birds brought them so much joy and laughter that every night when they said their prayers, the lady and the girl would forget all about the extra work and thank God for bringing the little feathered pair into their lives.

To this day they all are living happily ever after!

The End :)

# About the Author

*Clem and Nellie* is D. L.'s debut book. She hopes to write more that include Arianna, her adult daughter with special needs.

D. L. has had a challenging life and through the course of it has come to seek to rely on God no matter what comes her way. Her faith was thoroughly tested when her oldest son, Tim, died suddenly in 2017. Looking back, she sees that God carried her through that devastating experience and used it to deepen her relationship with Him.

This book came to be because D. L., a lifelong animal lover (especially dogs and ducks!), was attacked by a dog while delivering mail as a city letter carrier in May of 2022. She suffered a traumatic hand injury to her dominant hand that changed her life. D. L. loved her job delivering mail because it connected her to the community, and she felt she was able to be of service to the people on her route. The injury and the sudden loss of her ability to work the job she loved so much left D. L. feeling a bit lost and without purpose.

As the severity of the injury began to sink in, D. L. asked God to show her something meaningful she could do with the extra time she now had. Much to her surprise, she kept hearing, "Write a book," so when she could no longer ignore it, she did! :)

D. L. hopes to write other books that will be true stories about her daughter Arianna being brave and facing fears that are common among special needs people.

She also hopes that the writing of these books will demonstrate to anyone who struggles with life that when we sincerely want help and are willing to take action, God can take our lives to places we never dreamed possible.

With heavy hearts in September of 2023 ,D.L. and her family said goodbye to their German Shepherd Natasha who is featured in this book. She will be loved and missed forever.

D.L lives in Woodland California with her husband Michael, her daughter Arianna, their dog Rosie, kitty Solomon, and of course their beloved birds Clem and Nellie.

**And we know that ALL things work together for good to those who love God, to those who are called according to His purpose. (Romans 8:28)**

Printed in the USA
CPSIA information can be obtained
at www.ICGtesting.com
CBHW062130110724
11458CB00020B/187